True-Life Pirates

Mary Read and Anne Bonny

Cavendish
Square
New York

Rebecca Stefoff

Published in 2015 by Cavendish Square Publishing, LLC
243 5th Avenue, Suite 136, New York, NY 10016

First Edition

Website: cavendishsq.com

This publication represents the opinions and views of the author based on his or her personal experience, knowledge, and research. The information in this book serves as a general guide only. The author and publisher have used their best efforts in preparing this book and disclaim liability rising directly or indirectly from the use and application of this book.

CPSIA Compliance Information: Batch #WW15CSQ

All websites were available and accurate when this book was sent to press.

Library of Congress Cataloging-in-Publication Data

Stefoff, Rebecca, 1951-
Mary Read and Anne Bonny / Rebecca Stefoff.
pages cm. — (True-life pirates series)
Includes bibliographical references and index.
ISBN 978-1-50260-201-5 (hardcover) ISBN 978-1-50260-200-8 (ebook)
1. Read, Mary, -1720? 2. Bonny, Anne, 1700- 3. Women pirates—Caribbean Sea—Biography. I. Title.

G537.R43S74 2015
972.9'030922—dc23
[B]

2014019947

Editorial Director: David McNamara
Editor: Andrew Coddington
Copy Editor: Cynthia Roby
Art Director: Jeffrey Talbot

Senior Designer: Amy Greenan
Senior Production Manager: Jennifer Ryder-Talbot
Production Editor: Sam Cochrane
Photo Research: J8 Media

The photographs in this book are used by permission and through the courtesy of: Cover photo (beach), Denis Burdin/Shutterstock.com; Cover photo and 1, (engraving), Hulton Archive/Getty Images; Sergiy Zavgorodny/Shutterstock.com, 1 (woman); Embleton, Ron/ © Look and Learn/Bridgeman Images, 4; Herman Moll/Geographicus Rare Antique Maps/File:1732 Herman Moll Map of the West Indies and Caribbean -Geographicus - WestIndies-moll-1732.jpg/Wikimedia Commons, 7; Print Collector/Hulton Archive/Getty Images, 9; Howard Pyle/ File:Pyle pirate handsome.jpg/Wikimedia Commons, 11; Roger Viollet/Getty Images, 12; Earthquake at Port-Royal/© British Library Board/ Bridgeman Images, 15; Interfoto/SuperStock, 16; Frank E. Schoonover/Paine, Ralph Delahaye/File:Blackbeard, Buccaneer - Cover.jpg/ Wikimedia Commons, 18; Private Collection/Peter Newark Historical Pictures/Bridgeman Images, 20; Culture Club/Hulton Archive/ Getty Images, 21; Unknown, style of Sir Godfrey Kneller/Sir Gawain/File:Daniel Defoe Kneller Style.jpg/Wikimedia Commons, 23; Beauford, William/Bridgeman Images, 25; Hulton Archive/Print Collector/Getty Images, 26; William Hogarth/File:Rogers,Woodes.jpg/ Wikimedia Commons, 29; Culture Club/Hulton Archive/Getty Images, 30; Private Collection/Peter Newark Historical Pictures/ Bridgeman Images, 32; Hulton Archive/Getty Images, 33; John Warburton Lee/ SuperStock, 34; Culture Club/Hulton Archive/Getty Images, 38.

Cover and interior design elements: (pirate map) Vera Petruk/Shutterstock.com; (rope on old paper) Irina Tischenko/Hemera/ Thinkstock; (skull and crossbones) Tatiana Akhmetgalieva/Shutterstock.com; (crossed swords) Fun Way Illustration/Shutterstock.com; (old map elements) Man_Half-tube/iStock Vectors/Getty Images; (pirate flag) fdecomite/File:Pirate Flag (6084517123).jpg/ Wikimedia Commons; (ship) Makhnach_S/Shutterstock.com; (anchor) File:Anchor Pictogram.svg/Wikimedia Commons.

Printed in the United States of America

TRUE LIFE PIRATES

Contents

The Real Pirates of the Caribbean

On an October day in 1720, a ship commanded by Captain Jonathan Barnet sailed past the westernmost end of Jamaica, a hilly, forested island in the Caribbean Sea. That western tip of Jamaica is called Negril Point. Today it is dotted with resorts and vacation homes, but in 1720 it was nothing more than a sandy spit of land stretching from the island out into the clear, blue tropical water.

As he neared the point, Barnet heard a gunshot. It came from a nearby **sloop**, or a ship with one mast, like Barnet's own vessel. The

Mary Read and Anne Bonny fought alongside the men in their pirate crew.

strange sloop was not under sail, but anchored in place. The shot roused Barnet's curiosity, though, for he was no ordinary captain. He was a **privateer**, or a captain on a special mission from his government.

At the time, one of the most powerful figures in the Caribbean was Woodes Rogers. He was the governor of the Bahamas, a group of islands in Caribbean that was a **colony** of Great Britain, just as Jamaica was. Rogers had sent Barnet out to hunt pirates, especially the pirate known as John or Jack Rackam. Rogers had labeled Rackam and his crew "Pirates and Enemies to the **Crown** of Great Britain."

Barnet changed course to approach the anchored sloop. The threatening appearance of Barnet's vessel, armed with many cannons, must have alarmed the people aboard the sloop. They quickly raised their anchor and started to sail away. Barnet chased the sloop and caught up with it around ten o'clock that night. He called out, asking who was in command.

"John Rackam of Cuba!" came the answer. It was the pirate Barnet had been hunting!

Barnet ordered Rackam to surrender. In response, the pirates aimed one of their cannons at Barnet's ship. Barnet ordered his crew to fire at once. Their shots struck Rackam's sloop and ripped away the boom, or the piece of wood at the bottom of a ship's sail that holds the sail open and lets it move to catch the wind. Without the boom, the pirates could not steer their ship. They were helpless in the water.

A 1732 map shows Caribbean islands and mainland colonies claimed by European nations. Jamaica is the small pink island in the center.

Barnet pulled alongside the pirate craft, and his men swarmed aboard its deck. The pirates surrendered without putting up a fight—except for two of them. Those two furiously waved their swords and pistols. They shouted at the other pirates, urging them to resist Barnet and his privateers. They failed and were taken prisoner along with Rackam and the rest of his crew.

The two who put up a fight were no ordinary pirates. Their names were Mary Read and Anne Bonny. Few women have left their mark in the history of **piracy**, but Read and Bonny were notorious among the real-life pirates of the Caribbean.

The Rise of Caribbean Piracy

The Caribbean Sea is part of the Atlantic Ocean between North and South America. The western border of the Caribbean is made up of Mexico and Central America. Its eastern edge is a string of islands. Some of those islands, like the Bahamas, are sandy and flat. Others, like Puerto Rico and Cuba, have mountains and thick forests.

The first part of America that Christopher Columbus spotted on his historic voyage in 1492 was a Caribbean island, probably San Salvador in the Bahamas. He claimed that island, and others that he later visited, for Spain. His voyage was just the beginning. Soon ships from many European nations were sailing to the Caribbean.

One by one the islands were claimed by various European nations, including Spain, France, the Netherlands, and England. The first country to establish colonies was Spain. Some of the Spanish colonies were on islands, including Puerto Rico and Cuba. Other colonies, such as Mexico, Panama, and Colombia, were on the mainland.

Over the years, many of the colonies in and around the Caribbean changed hands when the nations of Europe fought among themselves. Jamaica is just one example. Columbus claimed Jamaica for Spain when

European nations frequently fought each other on land and sea, both in Europe and in the Americas.

he landed on the island in 1494. Its capital was the settlement of St. Jago de la Vega, located where the parish of St. Catherine stands today. Then, in 1655, Jamaica changed hands when England captured the island from Spain. After that time St. Jago was called Spanish Town by the island's English-speaking colonists. Rackam and his crew, including Mary Read and Anne Bonny, would one day face British justice in a court in Spanish Town.

Almost as soon as Europeans started exploring and colonizing the Caribbean, other Europeans started preying on their ships and towns. Some of the raiders' first targets were on the mainland, not the islands. Spanish settlements and ports dotted the coasts of Central and South America. This network of settlements on the mainland came to be called the Spanish Main.

The Spanish Main drew Spain's enemies like a magnet. Again and again they looted vast fortunes in silver and gold that the Spanish were taking from mines in their colonies. Raiders and pirates attacked

The Buccaneers

One of Spain's first colonies in the Caribbean was the large island of Hispaniola. Today, the island is divided between the countries of Haiti and the Dominican Republic. Hispaniola was settled by Spanish adventurers and colonists. When Spain destroyed a French settlement on the Florida coast in 1565, some of the French survivors fled to the island. They hid from the Spanish in Hispaniola's rugged, wooded hills. Over time they were joined by others who wanted to escape from the Spanish authorities.

Living in pairs or small bands, these outcasts survived by hunting wild animals. From the Native people of Hispaniola they learned to preserve meat by smoking it over fires on frameworks or grills made of wood. The Native people called these frameworks *buccans*. The hunters became known as *boucaniers*, which is French for "men who use *buccans*." The English called them **buccaneers**.

In the 1620s, the Spanish tried to drive the buccaneers out of Hispaniola. They did not succeed, but some of the buccaneers stole boats and moved to the small island of Tortuga, just off Hispaniola's northern coast. They turned from hunting and

The French settlers in the Caribbean who turned to piracy became known as buccaneers, the first pirates of the Caribbean.

general outlawry to piracy. Their method was to follow a passing Spanish ship under the cover of darkness, slip aboard, and use force to seize the ship and its **cargo**, often with great cruelty toward the Spanish crew. In the seventeenth century, "buccaneer" became another name for "pirate" in the Caribbean.

The buccaneers were originally French, but they were joined by runaway slaves, adventurers, criminals, and would-be pirates from many nations. Soldiers and sailors who deserted their posts, or who were left high and dry when military campaigns ended, joined them as well. The buccaneers formed a rough society of their own. Some called themselves "the brethren of the coast."

Men sign up to receive letters of marque from the governor, hoping to become lawful pirates, or privateers.

Spanish settlements on land and Spanish ships at sea. A prime target was the huge treasure ships, or **galleons**, that carried money and other valuables to and from Spain's colonies.

War and Privateering

Attacks and robberies carried out by sea captains and their crews were unlawful acts of piracy. Sometimes, though, what looked like piracy was not just legal, it could be positively patriotic! When two nations were at war, ships belonging to citizens of one nation could attack and loot ships or settlements of the other nation. It was legal as long as the attacking captain had an important piece of paperwork from his government called a **letter of marque**.

A letter of marque was sometimes called a commission or a license. These papers turned a captain into a privateer with permission from his government to attack an enemy ship and seize its cargo. Privateering was lawful only during wartime. It was also lawful only if the privateer's **prize**, or the ship that was captured or the settlement that was attacked, belonged to the enemy.

Privateers sometimes committed acts of piracy, seizing prizes that did not belong to enemy nations. On the other hand, pirates sometimes claimed to be privateers, hoping this would keep them from being hanged as pirates. In reality, the difference between pirates and privateers could be hard to determine. A good example is the career of Francis Drake of England. To the Spanish, he was a dreaded outlaw. To the English, he was a national hero.

In 1572 and 1573 Drake attacked ports on the Spanish Main. Since England and Spain were not at war at the time, Spain accused Drake of piracy. Queen Elizabeth I of England disapproved of what Drake had done, and he had to go into hiding.

In 1577, though, the queen secretly helped pay for Drake's next voyage against the Spanish in America. Calling himself a privateer, Drake seized the Spanish treasure galleon *Nuestra Señora de la Concepción* and its rich cargo that included tons of silver. Even though England and Spain were still not officially at war, tension between the two countries was high. This time the queen did more than approve of Drake's actions; she made him a knight.

Later, from 1585 to 1604, England and Spain were at war. Sir Francis Drake attacked the Spanish Main in 1586, but this time he really was a privateer, with a letter of marque from the queen.

Pirate Strongholds

One of the first pirate strongholds in the Caribbean was the buccaneer island of Tortuga. By the 1640s, the buccaneers had driven out the last of the Spanish settlers there. Pirate ships from all nations made the island their center of operations. Tortuga was small and soon became crowded. A new pirates' paradise appeared in 1655, when England took over the Spanish colony of Jamaica.

After England forced the Spanish out of Jamaica, it welcomed the buccaneers, who also considered themselves enemies of Spain. Port Royal, the English capital of Jamaica, became home base for many buccaneers.

The buccaneers raided a number of Spanish towns in the 1660s. Often their raids were planned and commanded by English military officers, who trained the buccaneers to fight like soldiers. At this time many of the buccaneers saw themselves as privateers, not pirates. The English government agreed. Henry Morgan was a ruthless buccaneer but also a successful privateer. He was made a knight and the lieutenant-governor of Jamaica as a reward for his attacks on Spanish towns.

By 1680, Port Royal had become a large and wealthy city, largely due to fortunes that had been won through piracy. England's view of

When an earthquake devastated Port Royal in 1692, some people said that the pirates were to blame.

the buccaneers had changed, however. Piracy was now a serious threat to English ships as well as to Spanish ones, and English authorities were beginning to crack down on pirate activity in Jamaica.

A terrible earthquake struck Port Royal in 1692, killing as many as two thousand people. Some said it was punishment for the city's wicked pirate ways. By that time, though, most of the pirates of the Caribbean had already moved to new havens. Some made their **lairs** on islands off the coast of Carolina. Others went to the island of New Providence in the Bahamas. It was in New Providence that Mary Read and Anne Bonny crossed paths with John Rackam and joined his pirate crew.

two

Girls Who Grew Up to Be Pirates

H ow did Mary Read and Anne Bonny end up as pirates in the Caribbean? There is only one source of information about their early lives. Unfortunately, we have no way of knowing whether that information is true.

Everything we know about the early lives of Read and Bonny comes from a book called *The General History of the Robberies and Murders of the Most Notorious Pyrates*, published in 1724. Its author, Charles Johnson, tells of many famous pirates of the seventeenth and early eighteenth centuries, including Captain William Kidd, Bartholomew "Black Bart"

Two pirate ships with frightening flags in an illustration from the *General History*.

17

Edward "Blackbeard" Teach is one pirate whose story is told in the *General History*, a book that is not completely reliable.

Roberts, Edward "Blackbeard" Teach, and Mary Read and Anne Bonny. Mixed with the facts, however, are made-up stories, including some stories about pirates who never existed at all.

Some of the information in the *General History* is fairly reliable. It is backed up by other historical documents such as letters and court papers. Other parts of the *General History* are based on nothing more than Johnson's imagination. He includes things that he could not possibly have known about, such as detailed conversations that took place years earlier, or the thoughts of a dying man. He also weaves the stories of imaginary pirates together with stories about real ones.

Certain parts of the *General History* cannot be labeled either "true" or "false." They may be fact, fiction, or something in between, a mix of truth, rumor, gossip, and imagination. What the *General History* says about Mary Read and Anne Bonny falls into the "mixed" group.

Historians know that Read and Bonny did exist, and that they were captured and tried as pirates. What the *General History* says about this part of their lives matches information from other sources. However, when the *General History* describes the childhoods and early lives of Read and Bonny, historians think that the author most likely made these stories up. There is no evidence to support them. Still, these stories are all we have.

Mary Read's Early Life

According to the *General History*, Mary Read was born in England, probably around 1691. Her mother had married a man who went to sea and did not return. After her husband's disappearance, she had a relationship with another man and became pregnant. She gave birth to a girl and named her Mary. Mary's mother had also had a son with her missing husband, but the boy died just before Mary was born. She thought that her dead son's grandmother might help pay for Mary's upbringing if she thought that Mary was her grandson. So Mary's mother disguised the little girl as a boy and passed Mary off as her dead brother.

From that point on, Mary Read was raised as a boy and known as Mark. She dressed in boy's clothes and, at the age of thirteen, got a job as a

Mary Read (left) is said to have fought another pirate to save the man she loved. True? No one knows.

footman, a male servant. Later she served as a sailor and then as a soldier, still passing as a man.

When Mary fell in love with a fellow soldier, she revealed her secret to him, and the two left the army and got married. Her husband later died. To support herself, Mary once again dressed as a man and became a soldier. She was on a ship bound for the Caribbean colonies when it was captured by pirates.

She then became a pirate, still passing as a man, and in 1719 she joined John Rackam's crew.

Anne Bonny's Early Life

Like Mary Read, Anne Bonny passed for a boy during her childhood. At least, that's what the *General History* says. She was born in Ireland in 1689. Her mother was a maid who worked for a lawyer and his wife.

Anne Bonny and Mary Read wore men's clothing when they were fighting.

Anne's father was the lawyer himself. The wife was so angry over her husband's relationship with the servant that she accused Anne's mother of stealing spoons. The accusation sent Anne's mother to prison. Anne's father then left his wife, taking Anne with him. He did not want people to know that she was his daughter, so he dressed Anne in male clothes. He told people that she was a boy training to become a lawyer's clerk.

In spite of the lawyer's secrecy, people gossiped about his broken marriage and his child with a servant. He went to America to start over, taking Anne with him. They settled in what is now South Carolina.

Anne's father became a successful merchant and landowner, yet Anne married a penniless sailor named James Bonny. Her father disowned her. The newlyweds then went to New Providence in the Bahamas to seek their fortunes as privateers. It was there that Anne met Rackam. In 1719 she left her husband and ran off with Rackam, joining his pirate crew.

Who Wrote the History of the Pirates?

When you think of pirates, do you think of buried treasure? Do peg legs and parrots spring to mind, or walking the plank? These and many more ideas about pirates also came from *General History of the Robberies and Murders of the Most Notorious Pyrates*. It was published in 1724, with a second volume in 1728.

Who was the author of this book about pirates? He called himself "Captain Charles Johnson," but that was just a pen name. His real identity remains a mystery today.

There was a writer named Charles Johnson in London at the time. He even wrote a play called *The Successful Pirate* that appeared on a London stage in 1713. However, he did not write the *General History*. Whoever wrote it probably used Johnson's name as a joke.

In 1932, an American scholar claimed to have solved the mystery of who wrote the *General History*. He claimed that the author was Daniel Defoe, who had already published the adventure story *Robinson Crusoe* and several novels about pirates. People agreed with this idea for more than fifty years. Then, in

Was the mysterious "Captain Johnson" really Daniel Defoe, author of *Robinson Crusoe*?

1988, two other literary researchers questioned the idea that Defoe was the author. They pointed out that there is no evidence linking Defoe to the *General History*. In addition, many things in the *General History* do not agree with the books that Defoe published under his own name.

Another idea is that the author of the *General History* was a man named Nathaniel Mist, a sailor who became a journalist and publisher. He had sailed in the Caribbean Sea and might have known a good deal about the pirates who were active there. Without definite evidence, though, the mystery will probably never be solved.

Earlier Female Pirates

Mary Read and Anne Bonny were not the first women to take up the pirate way of life. Although female pirates were not common, they did exist. One hundred and fifty years before Read and Bonny took to piracy with Rackam, several women became known as pirates in England and Ireland.

One such female pirate came from the Killigrew family, who lived in Cornwall in southwestern England, an area of rugged coasts with a history of piracy and smuggling. The Killigrews owned a lot of land and were part of the upper class. During the sixteenth century, however, several generations of the family either took part in piracy or supported pirates by providing them with ships and selling their **booty**.

Lady Mary Killigrew, who was active between 1530 and 1570, was the daughter of a pirate. She did not give up piratical ways after marrying into the Killigrew family. She not only sold stolen loot for pirates, but when a German ship entered a Cornwall harbor, she led the band of looters who boarded it to search for money it was rumored to carry. Lady Mary went to trial for this deed, but the jury was bribed and did not find her guilty.

Elizabeth Killigrew married Lady Mary's son John. She seems to have shared her mother-in-law's ideas about piracy. In 1582, after a storm drove a Spanish merchant ship to seek shelter in a harbor in Cornwall, Elizabeth Killigrew led an attack on the ship. For this act of piracy she was sentenced to hang, but a pardon from the king saved her life.

Pirate Grace Malley (left) meets Queen Elizabeth I. The two women met in real life.

Around the same time, an Irish woman became famous for her deeds at sea. Grace O'Malley was born around 1530 into an old Irish family that had several castles and a number of ships. The family businesses included fishing, trading, and piracy. Grace, who outlived two husbands, carried on the family business with her own fleet of as many as thirty ships.

O'Malley led raids against local rivals and also plundered merchant ships. The English governor in charge of the area where O'Malley lived called her a rebel and a traitor. He also arrested her son, although not for piracy. In 1593 O'Malley traveled to England to ask for help from Queen Elizabeth I, and the queen ordered her son released. Soon after that, Grace O'Malley retired from managing her fleet of ships. She died in 1603.

The lives of Mary Read and Anne Bonny were very different from those of the earlier female pirates. The Killigrews and O'Malleys owned land and ships. They were leaders with status in society. Mary Read and Anne Bonny were lower on the social ladder. If they hoped that piracy would improve their situations, they were wrong.

three

Sailing with Calico Jack

Mary Read and Anne Bonny were captured as pirates while sailing with John Rackam. Rackam was called "Calico Jack" because he liked to wear colorful clothes made of calico, a type of cotton cloth. Calico Jack's career as a buccaneer was short and not very successful. In fact, Rackam was a small-time pirate. He might be forgotten today if not for his connection with the two famous women pirates of the Caribbean.

"Calico Jack" Rackam was not much of a pirate. He is most famous for having women in his crew.

Rackam Becomes a Captain

We do not know much about the early life of John "Jack" Rackam (his name is spelled Rackham or Rackum in some sources). He shows up in the history of piracy in 1718, in the crew of pirate Charles Vane.

Vane and Rackam were Englishmen. Both men might have worked at sea on merchant ships or in the slave trade before they became pirates. Rackam was not just a member of Vane's crew, he was the ship's **quartermaster**. This was an important position. The quartermaster was an officer elected by the crew. He took charge of the pirates' booty when they looted another ship. Afterward, he guarded the booty and saw that it was properly shared out among the crew. On many pirate ships, the quartermaster had almost as much power as the captain.

In July 1718, Woodes Rogers came to the Bahamas as the new royal governor. He offered **amnesty**, or mercy, to any pirates who surrendered before September of that year. This meant that the government would pardon or overlook their crimes, as long as they stopped being pirates. Many of the buccaneers in New Providence took that offer and promised to give up their pirating ways.

Vane refused amnesty. Instead, he sailed away with his loot and his crew. They went north to the coast of South Carolina, where they captured several other ships. After a quarrel broke out between Vane and Rackam, the two went their separate ways. Rackam was given command of one of Vane's ships, and some of Vane's crew joined him.

Woodes Rogers (seated at right) and his family. Rogers both pardoned and pursued pirates.

Amnesty

Rackam was now captain of his own pirate vessel. By May of 1719, though, he was ready to give up the pirate life, or thought he was. Woodes Rogers once again offered amnesty to pirates who surrendered and agreed to work ashore. Rackam sailed to New Providence and accepted amnesty.

Some of the pirates who had taken amnesty discovered that they did not like building roads, clearing fields, and the other work the governor gave them. They broke their word and returned to piracy. This was

The Big Pirate Party

Edward Teach, known as Blackbeard, was a pirate who plundered ships in the Caribbean and off the coast of what is now the United States. In early 1718, he found a good hideout at Ocracoke Island, part of the maze of islands and waterways along the North Carolina coast. Other pirates visited Teach there to do business, share news, and sell their booty to the local settlers. In a short time the place became known as a pirate haven.

In October 1718, Charles Vane visited Teach at Ocracoke Island. Sixty or more pirates were on hand for a festival of drinking, carousing, and tale telling. It is not known for sure whether Calico Jack Rackam was present, but because he was Vane's quartermaster, he probably was. If so, he was part of what some historians say was the largest gathering of pirates in North America.

Blackbeard is said to have worn lit fuses in his beard to terrify his opponents.

dangerous. When Woodes Rogers heard of their plans, he had several pirates hanged along the waterfront.

In spite of the danger, Calico Jack Rackam soon grew tired of law-abiding life. On August 22 he and a dozen others rowed into the harbor and climbed aboard a sloop called the *William*, which belonged to a local man. The *William* had six cannons and a good supply of ammunition and food. Rackam and his crew quickly raised the anchor, spread the sails, and headed out to sea in the stolen craft. Mary Read and Anne Bonny were among those on board.

Women On Board

What was life like for the two women who sailed on the *William*? Details are rare. We do know that neither Read nor Bonny pretended to be men, as they had done earlier in their lives. Much of the time they wore women's clothes. Both were in relationships with fellow pirates. There were rumors that Bonny had a child with Rackam in 1719, and that they left the child with some friends of Rackam's in Cuba. As for Read, she became involved with a man in the crew.

When piratical deeds were called for, Read and Bonny did not hold back. They put on men's clothing and armed themselves with swords and pistols. Witnesses said that the two women took part in raids alongside the men, and that they were willing to do anything the male pirates did.

The two notorious women pirates of the Caribbean were said to fight even more fiercely than the men.

Turtles and Trouble

Governor Woodes Rogers was furious when Rackam, who had accepted amnesty, returned to his old ways and made off with the *William.* The governor declared that Rackam and his crew were criminals and enemies. It was no secret that two women had set sail on the *William.* The governor named Mary Read and Anne Bonny as members of the pirate crew. He promptly sent several ships out to search for Rackam.

Meanwhile, Rackam had attacked a few fishing boats in the Bahamas. When he heard that pirate hunters were after him, he sailed south.

A picture of one of the women pirates visiting her captain in prison—which almost certainly never happened.

The *William* took a few small prizes—local traders, mostly—near the islands of Hispaniola and Jamaica. None of these adventures brought much in the way of booty.

One day the *William* met a boat full of turtle hunters off Negril Point, Jamaica. The nine hunters came aboard the *William* to trade their turtle meat for rum, an alcoholic drink made from sugar. That's when Captain Jonathan Barnet, one of Governor Rogers's privateers and pirate hunters, caught up with the *William*. The unlucky turtle hunters had no chance to flee. They were taken prisoner along with the pirates, including Rackam, Read, Bonny, and the rest.

four

The Fate of the Female Pirates

The morning after Rackam and his crew were captured, Captain Barnet put them ashore on Jamaica. A British military officer took charge of them and marched them across the island to Spanish Town, where they were thrown into jail.

Two and a half months later, on November 16, 1720, John Rackam and ten of his male crewmen were tried for piracy. All were found guilty and sentenced to death. Six of the men were hanged in the town of Kingston, Jamaica. The other five were hanged near Port Royal, the English capital of Jamaica and a former pirate haven.

Rackam suffered a pirate's fate, and his body dangled in the harbor for months as a sign of the perils of piracy.

Rackam was one of those hanged near Port Royal. His body was placed in an iron cage that dangled from a tall post on an island in the harbor. Slowly rotting away, his body was meant to serve as a warning about the dreadful fate that awaited pirates.

A Surprise in Court

The trial of the women pirates was held on November 28, 1720. By that time Rackam and his crewmen were already dead. Read and Bonny knew that they could be facing the same fate.

Several witnesses gave evidence against the two women. These witnesses were people who had been on the ships that Rackam had attacked. One man said that Anne Bonny had handed gunpowder to the men. Another witness, a woman, said that Read and Bonny had threatened to kill her. All in all, the testimony of the witnesses made it clear that the women were not just passengers but participants in the pirate's attacks.

The court found Read and Bonny guilty of piracy and sentenced them to be hanged. Then the women said the one thing that could save their lives: "My lord, we plead our bellies." This was their way of saying that they were pregnant. The law would not hang a pregnant woman, because her unborn child was innocent.

Mary Read and Anne Bonny were both in fact pregnant, and so they escaped being hanged. Instead they were put into prison. Read became ill soon afterward and died in prison. Records show that she was buried in Jamaica in April 1721. Her child is not mentioned. No one knows whether

THE
TRIALS
Of Eight Perſons
Indited for Piracy &c.

Of whom **Two** were acquitted,
and the reſt found **Guilty**.

At a Juſticiary Court of Admiralty Aſſembled and Held in
Boſton within His Majeſty's Province of the Maſſachuſetts-
Bay in New-England, on the 18th of **October** 1717.
and by ſeveral Adjournments continued to the 30th. Purſu-
ant to His Majeſty's Commiſſion and Inſtructions, founded
on the Act of Parliament Made in the 11th. & 12th of
KING **William** IIId. Intituled, *An Act for the
more effectual Suppreſſion of Piracy.*

With an **APPENDIX,**

Containing the Subſtance of their Confeſſions
given before His Excellency the Gover-
nour, when they were firſt brought to
Boſton, and committed to Goal.

Boſton :
Printed by **B. Green,** for **John Edwards,** and Sold
at his Shop in King's Street. 1718.

The published records of piracy trials were popular reading at the time.

it died with her or was born and survived.

The fate of Anne Bonny and her child is another mystery. There is no record of her death. According to one traditional story, her father paid to have her released from prison, and she moved back to South Carolina with her child. Some researchers say that she may have returned to piracy, using a different name. Unfortunately, there is no proof of either story.

Legends and Fiction

In terms of treasure and glory, Mary Read and Anne Bonny were pretty poor pirates. Their pirating careers were short, and their loot was more likely to be turtle meat than gold doubloons. But they have gained a lot of fame over the centuries because there have not been many women pirates. The story of Read and Bonny has captured the imaginations of people from their own time to the present.

An American Woman Pirate

Rachel Wall was hanged in Boston, Massachusetts, in 1789. The crime for which she was tried and executed was robbery. She had tried to steal another woman's bonnet, a type of hat. At her trial, however, Wall claimed that she would rather be tried as a pirate.

Born around 1760 in Pennsylvania, Rachel married an American pirate named George Wall. He used trickery to capture other vessels. Wall would sail a small ship called a schooner, usually used for fishing, into a harbor and wait until a storm blew over. After the storm, he and his crew would mess up the sails to make it seem that the ship had been damaged in the storm. They would then raise a distress flag, asking for help. Rachel would stand alone on the deck, looking like the only survivor of a disaster. When another ship approached to offer help, Wall and his crew would seize it.

They stole cargoes, sank ships, and killed twenty-six people this way during 1781 and 1782. One storm proved to be too big for them, though. It wrecked their schooner, and Wall and one of his men died.

Rachel survived and returned to life on land, working as a servant. Faced with death for the crime of robbery, she admitted that she had been a pirate, but she had never stolen that bonnet.

Some people admire Read and Bonny for being strong enough to survive in a man's world, or for being bold enough to follow a most unladylike way of life. Others feel sympathy for these two women who did not seem to fit into the narrow, limited choices that were available to women of their day. Read and Bonny claimed the freedom to act independently and do what they wanted to do, as men did. At the same time, however, the paths they followed led them to a life of crime. The rewards were small, and the punishments were great.

Mary Read and Anne Bonny have been the inspiration for several works of fiction. The 1951 movie *Anne of the Indies* was supposed to be based on the life of Anne Bonny, although the character's name is Anne Providence. The story told by the movie, however, has little resemblance to Bonny's real history.

Characters named Anne Bonny have appeared in the television series *Black Sails* and in the videogame *Assassin's Creed IV: Black Flag*. The game also includes Mary Read, Jack Rackam, and Blackbeard. Like most books, films, television shows, and games about pirates, these entertainments contain much more fiction than fact. However, they point to the fact that pirate tales remain popular. People are eager to imagine the daring, adventurous, rip-roaring life of a pirate who escapes the dullness of everyday life to live wild and free on the sea. Mary Read and Anne Bonny may have found a kind of freedom as pirates, but buccaneering was dangerous, difficult, and often deadly, for women as well as for men.

Timeline

1530–1600 The Killigrew family, including Lady Mary and Elizabeth Killigrew, are active as pirates and supporters of pirates.

1582 Elizabeth Killigrew leads an attack on a Spanish ship in English waters.

1550s–1590s Grace O'Malley of Ireland earns a reputation as a raider and pirate.

ca. 1682 John Rackam is born in England.

1689 Anne Bonny is born in Ireland.

ca. 1691 Mary Read is born in England.

1690s Caribbean pirates begin using New Providence island in the Bahamas as a haven.

1718	Rackam is an officer on the ship of pirate Charles Vane; he takes over the ship with the approval of the crew; Woodes Rogers becomes the first royal governor of the Bahamas.
1719	Mary Read and Anne Bonny join Rackam's crew.
1720	The Royal Navy captures Rackam and his crew, including Read and Bonny; Rackam is hanged on November 18.
1721	Mary Read dies in prison; nobody knows what happened to Anne Bonny.
1724	*General History of the Robberies and Murders of the Most Notorious Pyrates* is published.
1789	Rachel Wall is hanged for piracy.

Glossary

amnesty A pardon for crimes or misdeeds, or an agreement that the government will overlook or forgive them.

booty The money, treasure, merchant goods, or other loot obtained by piracy.

buccaneer A pirate who was active in the Caribbean; from the Native American word *buccan* or *boucan*, meaning "a wooden grill for smoking meat," which the French turned into *boucanier*, a backwoodsman or hunter.

cargo The goods or merchandise stored on a ship for transport.

colony A territory outside a country's borders that is claimed, controlled, or settled by that country.

crown A general term for a monarch or royal government, as in "the English crown."

galleon A large oceangoing ship, with several masts and several decks, often used to carry large amounts of cargo.

lairs A resting or sleeping place or a hideout.

letter of marque The document that makes a sea captain a privateer by giving permission to attack ships belonging to enemy nations; may also be called a commission or a license.

piracy Unlawful attacks on or robbery of ships or property by sea captains and their crews.

privateer A sea captain who has a letter of marque authorizing attacks on enemy ships.

prize A ship captured at sea.

quartermaster A petty officer who is responsible for sending signals, for assisting with steering the ship, and for keeping track of the supplies and booty.

sloop A sailing boat with one mast.

Find Out More

Books

Gilkerson, William. *A Thousand Years of Pirates*. Plattsburgh, NY: Tundra Books, 2010.

Krull, Kathleen. *Lives of the Pirates*. New York, NY: HMH Books for Young Readers, 2010.

Yolen, Jane. *Sea Queens*. Watertown, MA: Charlesbridge, 2010.

Websites

Anne Bonny

www.charlestonpirates.com/anne_bonney.html

This biography of Anne Bonny focuses on her connection with South Carolina and is based on the *General History of the Robberies and Murders of the Most Notorious Pyrates.*

A Brief History of Piracy

www.royalnavalmuseum.org/info_sheets_piracy.htm

The Royal Naval Museum of Great Britain explains what piracy is with a short overview of the history of pirates.

Caribbean Piracy

public.gettysburg.edu/~tshannon/hist106web/Caribbean/Andrew.html

This page is an illustrated overview of the beginning and growth of piracy in the Caribbean.

The History of the Buccaneers

www.thewayofthepirates.com/history-of-piracy/buccaneers.php

The Way of the Pirates website features a short history of piracy in the Caribbean, with links to additional articles about buccaneers and female pirates.

Museums

The New England Pirate Museum

www.piratemuseum.com/pirate.html

Located in Salem, Massachusetts, this museum features a walking tour through the world of pirates, including recreations of a dockside village, ship, and a cave. Also on display are authentic pirate treasures.

The St. Augustine Pirate and Treasure Museum

www.thepiratemuseum.com

This interactive museum covers 300 years of pirate history, and boasts many artifacts including pirate loot, a real treasure chest, and one of only three surviving Jolly Roger flags.

Bibliography

Abbott, Karen. "If There's a Man Among Ye: The Tale of Pirate Queens Anne Bonny and Mary Read." Smithsonian.com, August 9, 2011. www.smithsonianmag.com/history/if-theres-a-man-among-ye-the-tale-of-pirate-queens-anne-bonny-and-mary-read-45576461/?no-ist.

Cordingly, David. *Under the Black Flag: The Romance and Reality of Life among the Pirates.* New York, NY: Random House, 2013.

Druett, Joan. *She Captains: Heroines and Hellions of the Sea.* New York, NY: Simon and Schuster, 2001.

Konstam, Angus, with Roger Michael Kean. *Pirates: Predators of the Seas.* New York, NY: Skyhorse Publishing, 2007.

Rogozinski, Jan. *Pirates!* New York, NY: Facts On File, 1995.

Travers, Tim. *Pirates: A History.* Stroud, UK: Tempus Publishing, 2007.

Index

Page numbers in **boldface** are illustrations.

About the Author

Rebecca Stefoff has written books for young readers on many topics in history, science, exploration, and literature. She is the author of the six-volume series Is It Science? (Cavendish Square, 2014) and the four-volume series Animal Behavior Revealed (Cavendish Square, 2014). Although she has scuba-dived in sunken shipwrecks in the Atlantic Ocean and the Caribbean Sea, she has yet to see her first pirate ship. You can learn more about Stefoff and her books for young people at www.rebeccastefoff.com.